How To Build A Log Cabin

By Rob Winters

✓ The Smart DIY Log Cabin Guide

Log Cabin Pro of 30 Years Reveals How To Build A Log Cabin Yourself... And SAVE THOUSANDS!

How To Build A Log Cabin

Copyright© 2006 - 2014 by Rob Winters

All rights reserved. No part of this publication may be reproduced, distributed, or transmitted in any form or by any means, including photocopying, recording, or other electronic or mechanical methods, without the prior written permission of the publisher, except in the case of brief quotations embodied in critical reviews and certain other non-commercial uses permitted by copyright law. For permission requests, write to the publisher, addressed: "Attention: Rob Winters," at the address below.

HANDSCO

Attention: Rob Winters

519 Blair Blvd. Forsyth, MO. 65653

http://www.HowToBuildALogCabin.com

Contact: logpro1@gmail.com for info on other products and services offered by this author

Dedicated to The American Dream!

As our country continues to struggle with economical challenges... the "American Dream" and some of our basic goals in life are also in danger for those of us that work so hard for our Families. This Ebook Guide was created to offer some additional "light at the end of the tunnel" as it relates to those of you that have a goal of home ownership one day...and more precisely... the dream of building and owning a Log Cabin of your own! This is mainly for those of you that are "Do-It-Yourselfers" at heart, but is a great manual for all Log Cabin Fans!.

Many years ago in 1976, I visited a friend's newly constructed Log Cabin. I was instantly amazed at the sense of comfort, the pleasant smell of wood, the openness of design, and the beauty of the natural craftsmanship that was to be his dream home for years to come. I was hooked!. I began to study and learn everything I could about Log Homes, and began planning to build my first log home. Soon thereafter, This passion turned into a career of over 30 years in Log Home Construction. We hope that you will find the information you need here in this Ebook. If you don't... simply contact us and we will help all we can!

After over 30 years as a Log Home Pro ...I have learned all of the secrets that many builders won't tell a "Do-It-Yourselfer", and I have included them in this ebook!

In this book I want to show you that it is more than possible to build the Log Home or Retirement Cabin of your dreams yourself for a fraction of the cost of having a contractor build it!

Many have abandoned this dream because they thought they lacked what it takes to do much of the work themselves, and could not afford to have a "Pro" build their dream Log Home or Vacation Cabin for them.

All throughout my career I have been passionate about helping people achieve the dream of Log Home ownership… because there is nothing quite like it. But It has also been heart breaking at times to see Folks work so hard, and say "maybe someday".. But many have never been able to enjoy the warm relaxing atmosphere of a fire crackling in a stone fireplace, or the peaceful surroundings of beautiful natural wood logs in an open vaulted floor plan.

So… they simply gave up on their dream.

This should not happen to you! It is very do-able if you follow the right steps and follow your action plan!

Don't hesitate to Contact Us if you get stuck!

Email: logpro1@gmail.com

Best Regards,

Rob & Denise Winters

Table of Contents

Dedicated To The American Dream!

Introduction To The Log Cabin Lifestyle

Chapter 1 - It Starts With Your Dream!

Chapter 2 - Can You Really Build A Log Home Yourself?

Chapter 3 - Your Budget Guidelines

Chapter 4 - What About Financing A Log Home Or Cabin

Chapter 5 - Picking Your Home's Building Site

Chapter 6 - Choosing The Right Floor Plan

Chapter 7 - The Handcrafted Log Home

Chapter 8 - Choosing The Right Logs

Chapter 9 - Peeling Your Logs

Chapter 10 - Setting Your First Logs In Place

Chapter 11 - Notching Corners And Building Log Walls

Chapter 12 - Laying Out And Building Your Loft

Chapter 13 - Proper Roof Design

Chapter 14 - Building Your Roof System

Chapter 15 - All About Windows And Doors

Chapter 16 - Milled Log Home Options

Chapter 17 - The Advanced Handcrafted Or Hybrid Log Home

Chapter 18 - Choosing The Right Log Home Supplier

Chapter 19 - Log Home Finishes

Chapter 20 - Hvac Heating And Cooling Systems

Chapter 21 – Log Cabin Interior Design

Chapter 22 - A Rock Fireplace For Under $1000

Introduction To The Log Cabin Lifestyle

The log Home of the 21st century has evolved from the temporary shelters that pioneers used in the per-industrialized age of our country, to now becoming the ultimate retirement or primary residence for many in the "Baby Boomer" generation. The popularity of log homes has soared in the last 30 years, and many log home companies are building high quality Log Homes for this generation to choose from.

Your next question probably is…. **Should I build it myself? Or let an experienced builder do it for me?** This is where it becomes necessary for you to carefully consider your options. If you have the time, and don't mind being patient, If you don't mind a little hard work, and sweat equity, and if you don't mind taking the time and effort to look for bargains on building supplies and components.... then you may be able to build a home for under $50,000.00 But we'll cover that scenario a little while later. First let's look at a scenario with a builder's involvement.

"How do I know where to start with so many options, Log Home companies, and variations in construction costs?"

This is the reason why I wrote this book…. To make this sea of information, and all of these choices a whole lot easier to navigate through. I personally became a student of the Log Home Industry back in the mid 1970's, and soon thereafter, a Log Home builder. I have personally been involved in the construction, modification, and restoration of over 150 Handcrafted log Homes, Milled Log Homes, and Hybrid log Homes*. (Combination of "stick frame" and logs).

You say 150 homes is not that much…. Please don't confuse a "throw-it-up" stick built home, with a quality built, "one of a kind" log home structure.

While a log home does not need a millennium to build, it usually takes at least 50% more time to build if you are doing it right! So… Be cautious when some sales person or a builder tells you that a Log Cabin can be built in the same amount of time it takes to build a stick frame home. This is never quite the case. Even if your log home is built with a kit or milled Logs, it still requires some customized applications that can take more time.

If you are working with a good log home company and a competent builder, they will not rush the construction of your Log Cabin, but will cover all the bases and should move ahead with an average construction time period of between 9-16 months depending on what style of Log Home you are building.

I have personally been involved directly or indirectly with Log Homes ranging from 450 sq. ft. to 28,000 sq. ft. There are principal construction techniques applied to all of these Log Homes, with minimum standards of quality that must be followed & acceptable, to build a Log Home that any Homeowner or builder can be proud of.

If you find it hard to understand terminology used in this publication, I suggest that you click on "**Isometric Drawing**".

Here you will find a helpful tool that will illustrate every major component of a typical Log Home. If you build it right... you will enjoy the experience of your lifetime.

In this Book I am primarily focused on educating the average person interested in a planning guide for building a Log Home by doing most or all of the work themselves. I also have mentored a few builders who although very competent, did not have any experience in building with Logs. I know from experience that living in a well built log home can be a great lifestyle, and is a very comfortable home to live in!

So... by now you are asking...

How do I know if I am ready to fulfill my dream of building and owning a beautiful Log home? In the first chapter we'll start by qualifying you, and your individual needs that may relate to your Log home lifestyle!...

Chapter 1 - It Starts With Your Dream!

Quite often the reality of owning a dream log Home is the culmination of many years of planning and dreaming of the day you can start to live in that special place tucked back in the trees, by a lake, with deer playing nearby, a fire crackling in the fireplace, fresh bread baking in the oven….
Whoooo! Back the Truck up!... Ok…I was enjoying it also, but we are still in the planning stages.

Although I have lived this Log Home lifestyle, I have also experienced the blood, sweat, & tears on the path to get there as well.
But...If you access the right sources for up-to-date relevant information, you will one day stand on the porch of your very own quality built Log Home, and enjoy the satisfaction of being the proud owner of your very own cabin.

This book contains a list of things that need to be covered in order to realize a cost effective; and enjoyable experience along your journey to successfully building and living in your log Home.

First of all, take a hard look at your present lifestyle, and what goals you may have left to be reached. If you are at least willing to divert financial resources to your Log home project, then move ahead. If you are uncertain… then take the time to qualify if when you will have the time and money to move forward.

Here are some things to consider:

- Are you financially prepared to purchase your lake lot or country acreage?

- Can you afford to pay for at least 25% of the total cost of your log home project out of your own pocket, or from savings?

- Do you have the ability to dedicate the time & effort to co-ordinate with your builder all that is needed to keep things progressing along?

- Or...Will you be your own builder and commit yourself to the task of building your own log home?

These are all questions you need to ask yourself, to properly qualify where your personal commitment needs to be in the building process. Don't be afraid to wait until all of the ingredients for a successful building project are in place before you pull the trigger and get started.

In this Book we will try to help you qualify your personal involvement in the building of your own Log Cabin, as well as explore some options that you may never have considered!

Do not sell yourself short!... Many people well into their prime or (over 50), have successfully built their own Log home or Vacation Cabin, and have stayed well within a planned budget!

Stay focused on your plan!

Over the years many countless articles have been featured in all the log home magazines, and many described numerous frustrating episodes dealing with different issues during the course of building a Log Home. Builders can be blamed for some unexpected issues that arise during construction, but many times I have observed poor communication and planning on the part of the homeowner….. as the culprit. On the other hand...If you do not use a builder, you will enjoy the satisfaction of knowing intimately every detail of your Log Home, and the confidence that any challenge or problem can be solved with our expertise to back you, at very little cost.

What happens so often is that a homeowner will get what I call the "Gingerbread Glaze". This is what happens when a couple or individual constantly sees their dream in their minds and hearts, and become oblivious to budget and other important factors. They get carried away with throwing money at their dream, and do not carefully monitor budget shrink or cost swell. If you can afford to do this, then enjoy! But too often the inspiration factor creates a sense of justification for spending more than we planned, and we soon realize we are over budget, and in trouble.

So… it is very important that you are happy staying within the plan that you started with. Don't get carried away!! You can upgrade your project after you have had time to live in your home for a while, and can accurately determine which things are most important to you, or that you need to consider upgrades on.

This will avoid creating unnecessary frustration for both you and your builder. Builders will make changes for you, but you will be signing a lot of change order requests, and spending extra dollars on labor and materials. If that builder is to be you … then this applies all the more. (More on that later).

<u>Check with your local building inspector for any Code requirements to factor in.</u>

The Isometric Drawing link on our Web site will show you the basic anatomy of a Log Home:
http://www.theloghomeguide.com/isometric_drawing.html

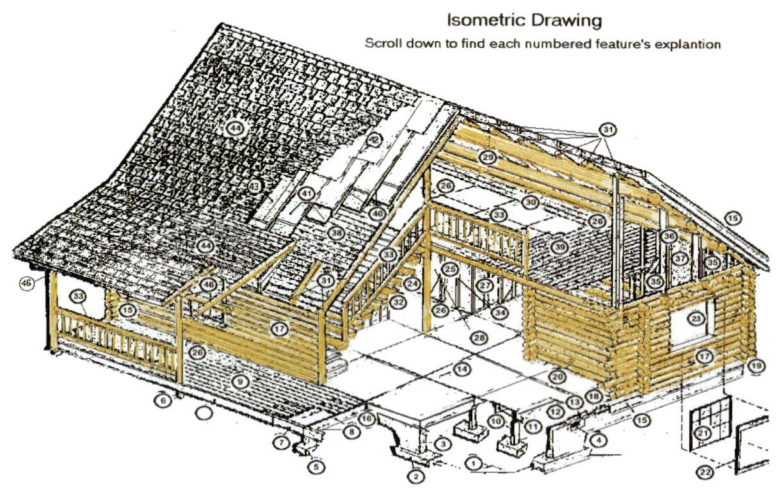

Chapter 2 - Can You Really Build a Log Home Yourself ?

The answer is: Of course you can !!!

Many people have done just that … it just takes a little education and determination. Do not sell yourself short!... Many people well into their prime or (over 50), have successfully built their own log home or vacation cabin, and have stayed well within a planned budget!
First of all try to determine if you feel comfortable doing any or all of the work yourself.
There are many good log home building schools available that offer from 2 days to a 1 week course and then 6-month courses as well...in Log Home construction. Most of the longer courses are geared for people who may want to make a career of Log Home Construction, and tuition will be expensive.

If you have the time to build your Log Home yourself... this is another option.

Remember… we can assist you every step of the way!

Email us: logpro1@gmail.com

I know this may seem scary to some of you ... but if done correctly, an Owner-built Log Home is affordable, and awesome to live in! They are simply one of a kind. This is the only type of log home construction that can either cost you the most to build... or the least to build. If you choose to get involved in 100% of the construction process yourself... the Handcrafted Log Home can provide you with the most immediate home equity value!

Click on the link below to look at some pictures of handcrafted log homes:
http://www.theloghomeguide.com/log-home-pictures

LOG HOME - Pictures

Whether you choose hands on approach or employ a builder, use this guide to your advantage. Building your Log Home yourself is a very cost effective way to greatly reduce the overall costs of building you own log home. If you have the time, and feel up to the challenge of trying to build a Log Home yourself, then I highly recommend this approach, as it will reward you in many ways. You will also need some tools that you may not have at this time. We can help you make sense of all of this.

The biggest pennies on the dollar way to save a ton of money is to build with "Raw Logs". This requires the most work but has a nice benefit to it. You will be building the "Handcrafted" Log Home, which is considered the most desirable, and beautiful form of Log Construction. And you will also build the best equity in your Log Home using this method!

You will need to first locate a Logger, or a Sawmill willing to sell you raw logs.

Today's prices for raw logs are around 35-60.00 per ton. For the average 1500 to 1800 Sq. Ft. Log Home you will need approximately (3.5) Log Truck Loads or approximately 100-120 Tons.

You will need to budget for logs that include your walls, Roof Support System, Support Posts, Loft Floor Joists and Stairs, etc. Bear in mind that many logs in your required list would be short enough to haul on a trailer with a 3/4 ton Pick-Up or larger. This will save you even more money! Also if you set up a gin pole with a DC electric winch (3-Ton or higher rating) you can set it up in the "just off center" position of your home using a straight log that can be used to support your loft, stairs, or another application. It will need to lift your Ridge Beam (the highest point) as well as log walls, floor joists, and purlins (roof support Beams), so it will need to be approx. 10' higher than your ridge beam to give you room for your rigging and winch to work.

Click on this link for more info on building a Gin Pole:
http://www.logbuilding.org/GinPoles.ch5.pdf

or ...email us for the .PDF if this link ever fails.

Chapter 3 - Your Budget Guidelines

Worksheet (example for staying under $50,000.00)

NOTE: We have included a link to a Bonus included called Log Home Costs It is a pdf file that will be a great tool for you to use in budgeting your construction costs.

This is merely a guideline to help you stay within a Cost effective Budget for building your Log Home or Vacation Cabin. These costs may vary some depending on how you build, What style of Construction you use, how much of the construction you actually do yourself, and what materials and components your use to build with.

For this example we will use the "PINECREST CHALET"

Click here to view the **"PINECREST CHALET"** :
http://www.theloghomeguide.com/pinecrest-chalet.html

The first floor has 936 sq. ft the second floor has 615 sq. ft.

This floor plan won a national award for it's overall design!

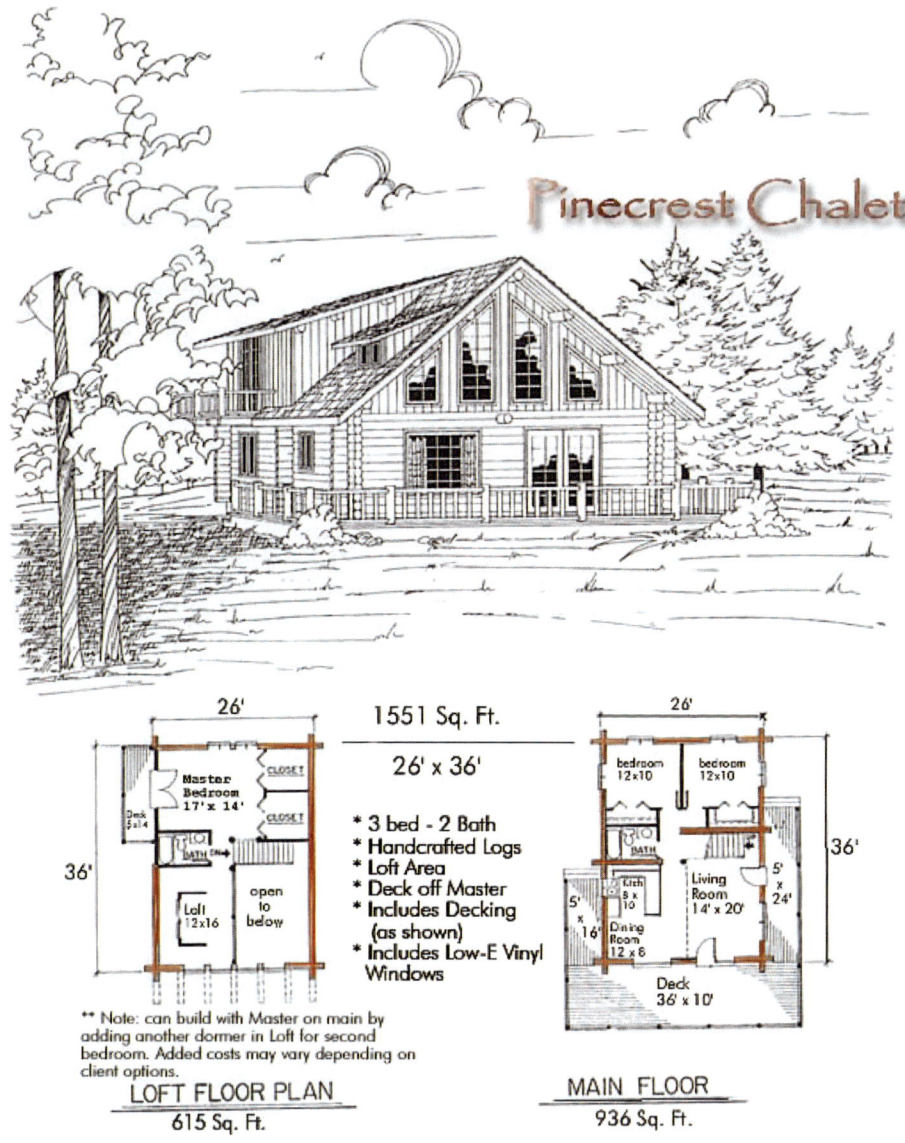

Pinecrest Chalet

1551 Sq. Ft.

26' x 36'

* 3 bed - 2 Bath
* Handcrafted Logs
* Loft Area
* Deck off Master
* Includes Decking (as shown)
* Includes Low-E Vinyl Windows

** Note: can build with Master on main by adding another dormer in Loft for second bedroom. Added costs may vary depending on client options.

LOFT FLOOR PLAN
615 Sq. Ft.

MAIN FLOOR
936 Sq. Ft.

Chapter 4 - What About Financing a Log Home or Cabin

NOTE: Below is a list of potential lenders specializing in or at least more familiar with Log Home Loans:

https://www.mtb.com/personal/Pages/Index.aspx
http://www.e-farmcredit.com/default.aspx?5-1063
http://www.logloans.com
http://www.nva-mortgage.com/log_home_financing.htm

In the past 30 years many banks, and mortgage lenders, have come to see the value in underwriting Log Home loans. With the trends for Log Home purchases rising consistently, the equity values of most well built log homes are attractive to lenders. Also... the average log home buyer is more financially stable than those in the much bigger conventional home market. Realtors have no problem selling a well built log home, so Lenders see it as a lower risk investment.

Also interest rates are lower dollar for dollar than conventional stick built homes, due to this group of borrowers. You should check with your own lender first to see if they will quote you a good interest rate for your Log Home loan.

If you have never built a home before, you need to know that there are two loans involved. The first one will be your construction loan, and it usually carries a bit higher interest rate than the long-term mortgage. This is carried generally from 6-9 months, or until your project is completed, and you are ready to move into your new Log Home. When the first lender has signed off on the completed Log Home, then generally an additional lender, or the same one will take over and carry the long term mortgage over the next 15-30 years.

Here are some pricing guidelines that reflect a regional trend in those areas. Don't be scared by the prices you see below, because there are ways to avoid having to pay those costs per sq. ft.

NOTE: While a cost per sq. ft is not an accurate way to estimate construction costs due to so many variables… It can be a good benchmark to use for planning purposes. Most good builders will not just quote you a cost per sq. ft. and let it go at that. They may use that to get you in the "ball Park" but, should use a much more complete costing matrix to arrive at your construction costs.

If you become more involved in the construction process, you can knock these costs down.

If you plan smart…

You can build a log home for around 40-50.00 per sq. ft. … providing you are willing to do 90% of the work yourself. (This does not include the cost of your Land)

If you have financial resources to have your log dream home built for you, then here is some helpful information:

Today studies show that the following cost trends are pretty accurate for new custom home construction costs per sq. ft. in various regions of the US.

***These prices will reflect no sweat equity from you the homeowner, other than the need to communicate well with your builder.

West Coast States Region …………..........175.00 - 250.00 per sq. ft.
Rocky Mountain States Region ……….....150.00 - 250.00 per sq. ft.
Central Midwest States Region………....110.00 - 150.00 per sq. ft.
North Eastern States Region ……....…...175.00 - 275.00 per sq. ft.
Southern States Region……………….....125.00 – 200.00 per sq. ft.

This is where we must talk about your budget. Yes… the "B" word.

If you have spent any time reading Log Home magazines, looking at pictures, reviewing log home brochures, by now you probably know what you want in a Log Home. The question is … can you afford it? You will need to carefully study your current lifestyle and determine what kinds of sacrifices you are willing to make for this dream to become a reality. It may come down to liquidating other assets or making other choices as this relates to building your Log Home. You may need to start buying components on sale or building in many small phases over time.

A word of caution here…Remember that building materials can be damaged by the elements, and you will want to be careful to stage each phase of construction so that you do not leave finished work exposed to the weather, and later face the need to tear up and replace what you have already installed.

Are there ways to build a Log Home on a smaller budget?   Yes!... this is very possible, but it requires more of a sweat equity commitment from you!

Chapter 5 - Picking Your Home's Building Site

Choosing your log home building site can be a lot of fun but is extremely important in many ways. This is where you will spend a lot of quality time enjoying the comfort of the Log Home lifestyle you dreamed of. You will want to avoid unnecessary added costs that a poor choice in building sites can add to your bottom line. Many will look for a lot or acreage and then walk their potential future home until they find a spot that "just feels right". OK... Many of us have made that soul connection with our "little piece of heaven" as well. But... you may not have considered some very important factors in avoiding extra costs... Big Costs!

Even if you plan to live there forever... You will want to choose the best building site for your Log Home or cabin for many reasons. The old saying: location...location...location, is very relevant in any real estate market. So carefully learning everything you can about the general area, what it's long term economic development plan is, what zoning changes may effect your property values, and what the expected increase in home equity values will be in coming years, are just a few of the most important factors when choosing the right building site for your new custom log home or cabin.

You will also want to consider excavation costs, drainage, driveway access, Electric power supply, and energy efficiency as well. It is widely accepted that a southwest exposure to the side of your home with the most windows is best. This may not always be possible but it will result in added savings each year in heating and cooling costs. The difference in costs savings can range from 350.00 to 1500.00 per year.

If you plan to build on a basement you will want to carefully consider good drainage, water tables, septic requirements, restrictions, Trends, etc. If you are considering a "walk-out" Basement site, you will need to consider installing an 18"- 24" wide drainage buffer or "French Drain" to insure that any water will have a way to be carried away from your basement walls. Your realtor should provide this information to you upon request. DO NOT attempt to pour a basement in a hole with (4) sides (or a subterranean basement). It has been the experience of most homeowners that this will likely cause flooding problems with this scenario. Stick with a (3) sided walkout basement with the drainage design above and you will avoid most of these problems. Spending a bit more to purchase land that has a building site that will require less "dirt work" and has less challenges with drainage issues, erosion, and septic, will save you potentially thousands in the long run.

What are your pre-development costs?

These costs refer to what it will take to get utilities installed, driveway or access road built, well and septic installation costs, and excavation costs for a foundation, etc. All these costs can vary so much that you will want to do some additional homework before committing to a home site purchase. Let me explain: If your proposed building site has solid rock as I have seen, you may need to blast just to get deep enough for a basement if you want one. This can be very expensive. Also you may need to get a perk test done to determine what kind of septic system will be required. You can spend the typical 2500.00 - 3500.00 on a normal septic system, or if your site is not suitable for that, it may require another type of system and those costs can reach $15,000.00 easily. Just be cautious and get written documentation from your realtor on these issues. Water Well costs can vary also if you need to drill very deep to find water. The water tables in some areas of our country are getting lower and lower. If you are in a low area you may need to go 150-200 ft. to get good water. If you are on a mountain or higher elevations, you may need to drill from 350 - 450 ft. or more to get good water. All these things need to be qualified as it relates to the asking price of the home site you are considering for purchase. **In short... Do your Homework!...** Once you have these issues behind you, and you have purchased your home site you can...Choose the right floor plan that properly fits your building site.

Check with your local building inspector for any Code requirements to factor in.

Chapter 6 - Choosing the Right Floor Plan

Take a look at all of the over 70 Log Cabin House Plans we have on our web site: http://www.logcabinhouseplans.net

Choosing a floor plan is very exciting and this is where the "Gingerbread Glaze" factor can cloud your judgment if you are not careful.

A few years ago, my folks wanted to build their own dream home. As the weeks turned into months my mother's drawings and plans changed from a moderately well designed home for two, into a sprawling monster that when finally built, was... way more home than they really needed. They realized a bit too late that a bigger commitment to maintenance, Heating and Cooling energy costs, and cleaning came with this much larger home. So be careful in choosing a Floor Plan that is right for you.

Most Log Homes are built with at least some exposure to a vaulted ceiling, which even for a 1200-1500 sq. ft. home can seem very spacious. I suggest that before you decide, go and tour some open houses to get a sense of the kind of space you feel comfortable with. Then your choices will become better defined. You will also want to consider how your floor plan fits on your building site.

Yet another consideration is the climate where you live. Choosing the right floor plan for your region will have some reasonable effect on your maintenance costs, heating & cooling costs, as well as initial construction costs if you need HVAC upgrades due to a complicated floor plan.

Choosing the correct size of logs is important whether you live in the northern or southern part of our country. Selecting logs with a minimum of 9" at the top and 12" at the butt end will give you an average mean diameter of 10.5" Because you will alternate the log ends while building your log shell... this will give you the desired R- rating to save a ton of money on Heating and Cooling costs. If you use any smaller logs... you will not get these saving using smaller logs, unless you are building a Log Cabin that is under 1200 SQ. FT.

Many Log Homes in the South have large porches for protection from the elements. Log Homes in the West follow more of the chalet style of construction. Wherever you live... keep in mind how your design will effect the home's optimum functionality. Boy... That's a mouth full! In any case choose a Floor Plan that is right for your family and your lifestyle. Don't be drawn in by a false "Television Show" standard that says a kitchen should cost $50,000.00 to be a full functioning kitchen.

I'm all for prosperity and the right for anyone to achieve their dream of having the best money can buy... but if you really don't need it, or do not have the means to support that desire... then simply be smart...be realistic, and enjoy a more debt free & stress free life!

This more careless kind of thinking is what has recently caused our country's leadership to make decisions that have created so much debt for us.

The Kitchen featured here is in a smaller Log Home but looks very nice. It cost approx. $4,000.00 for Cabinets, Appliances, Tile Flooring, and all. (Of course the homeowner provided all of the labor.)

Using the right combination of Logs and other woods is important to your overall look.

Designing the right Kitchen will give you many years of enjoyment!

Chapter 7 - The Handcrafted Log Home

By now you have probably noticed that I am a big fan of "Build-it-Yourself" Thinking! There are those of you that may still consider having a Custom Log Home or Vacation Cabin built for you, but we will cover construction styles before we talk about Log Home Companies to choose from.
If you have looked at many Log Home magazines you have already made some conclusions on what you like, and don't like. If you are still uncertain try to plan for a couple of weekend getaways in lodges or resorts that offer the styles of log home construction you are interested in. While a weekend will not give you concrete help in decision-making, you will experience the taste of different log home environments, which will help. It will also serve to give you inspiration for decorating your own Log Home. Next… send off for many different brochures, and begin to narrow down the Log Home Company candidates you are considering to supply you with your log home package.

Of my 30+ years of involvement in the Log Home Industry, most of that time was spent building Handcrafted Log Homes. Because of their mostly custom, handcrafted nature...they are the hardest to build, but in my opinion, the absolute most beautiful type of Log home construction there is. The Handcrafted Log Home has been the Log Home of choice for many folks on a budget, and the wealthy alike.

This style of construction is also known as Scandinavian, Swedish Cope, Full-Scribe, Traditional Chinker. There are some very good builders in this segment of our industry. This type of log home construction will also take the longest to finish, but you will have a one-of-a-kind log home as a result.

Now there are some things to consider ...

SETTLING & SHRINKAGE - You will need to allow for some settling & shrinkage, and you should use 2"x 2" angle iron key-ways for the window & Door bucks. let me explain...

This is the best system for settling. Don't be afraid of a handcrafted Log Home settling or shrinking some, because there are many ways to allow for it that do not effect the structural integrity, or create problems if the home is built right and you allow for some of this. <u>Settling Allowances</u> are normal and will need to be planned for.

NOTE: Anyone that advocates a "no shrinking/no settling" approach to a handcrafted log home is either naive, or is "**working against the grain**" because this approach has been the norm for centuries by highly skilled craftsman in many countries including Scandinavia where Log Home Construction was first mastered.

Plan for Settling and Shrinkage in the following areas:

- *Over windows and doors*
- *Interior framed partition walls*
- *Plumbing joints*
- *Your vertical support posts*
- *Fireplaces*
- *Any other applications where your log walls connect to Non-settling elements.*

The rule of thumb is to allow 1/2" to 3/4" for every foot of wall height when logs are somewhat Green. You should try to cut down or harvest your House Logs between October to March when the Sugars and Sap are at the lowest point.

This will help minimize shrinking and settling. You should plan to build with 9' walls. This allows for some settling and for upper level log floor joists that when notched in place, will be approx. half of their diameter lower than the wall logs at the lowest point.

Example: 9" Log floor joist will be 4.5" lower than top plate log in wall.

**NOTE:** There are products that are being touted by many for assisting in the settling process of a handcrafted Log home. They are spring loaded, and is designed to control and moderate settling. I can tell you that some areas of the country are requiring the use of them in the wall logs. This is an added unnecessary expense if you simply allow for proper settling in the first place. I have NEVER used them in over 30 years of building Handcrafted Log Homes and 90% of the homes I built were Handcrafted. I have NEVER had any settling problems in my homes!

Nevertheless... Check with your local building inspector for any Code requirements to factor in.

How long will it take to erect the Log Shell?

The Log Shell should be pre-assembled on a level open area such as an open field or pasture, to give you plenty of room to load and unload each log as you fit them together in the Pre-assembly Phase. This will take from 6-12 weeks depending on you, your tools, any outside help, and sheer determination. A "Chinker" is the easiest style since you are just notching the corners.

A "Full-Scribe"Log Home will take 40% longer to build the Log Shell. I have built some smaller Chinker Log Shells all by myself with no lifting machinery just dry cured logs, ingenuity, and brute strength, in less than 3 weeks. While I don't recommend this... it is possible if you are up to it.

Plan to invest in some lifting, and log handling equipment. While you could purchase a Tractor or Skid-Steer, you could also set up a gin pole for much less money and actually have a more versatile piece of equipment. A complete Gin Pole set-up should cost about $800.00 to 1200.00 (including a 3 ton electric 12 volt winch)

**Click on this link for more info on building a Gin Pole:**
http://www.logbuilding.org/GinPoles.ch5.pdf

Once the Log Shell has been pre-assembled, the re-assembly process should take about a week or less for most average sized Homes. You will need to Label & Mark each log on each course and round as you disassemble your Log Shell to make sure they go back together correctly when you re-assemble the Log Shell on it's Foundation/Sub floor.

It is also important to use wood brightener on your Log Shell if it has turned a bit dark during the pre-assembly process. This will save you some work later on when you begin to apply finishes to the Logs. A 50/50 Bleach & Water Solution also works, but make sure you scrub the logs good with clean water after letting stand for a half-hour or so.

Wiring - How to Wire a Log Cabin

After the Log Shell is completed at your pre-building location...You will want to pre-drill all rough wiring routing holes in the log yard as you begin to break down the pre-assembled Log Shell for shipment. If you are building on site... simply drill each routing hole in each log you build with as you are going up. Keep your wiring away from areas that will require re-bar or pipe dowels. (More on this in a bit)

NOTE: It is important that this is done so that you or your electrician will be able to quickly thread the Romax rough wiring through each log as each log course is laid. If there is any suspicion of the wiring being damaged while this routing is being done... You should do a continuity test. It is also a good idea to use PVC wiring chase tubing to route the wiring through. This will take a bit longer to accomplish, but it will further protect your wiring, and may be required in your area.

Check with your local building inspector for any Code requirements to factor in.

Re-bar or Pipe doweling

As you are building your Log shell you will need to plan for either 5/8" re-bar or pipe to use for connecting each log to the one above or below it. This is done so that any natural tendency for the logs to move sideways is eliminated. You will want to use re-bar or pipe at points approx. 1 foot away from each side of every door and window openings. alternate and offset drilling locations with every log and space re-bar drilling hole locations about 4" apart.

NOTE: When drilling for your re-bar or pipe locations... you will want to use an auger bit that is about 1/8" larger that the re-bar or pipe sections you are using. This is so the logs will settle or "drift" downward without binding up. Drill deep enough to go about halfway into the log below but cut your re-bar or pipe sections about 2" to 3" inches or so shorter.

NOTE: There are products that are being touted by many for assisting in the settling process of a handcrafted Log home. They are spring loaded, and is designed to control and moderate settling. I can tell you that some areas of the country are requiring the use of them in the wall logs. This is an added unnecessary expense if you simply allow for proper settling in the first place. I have NEVER used them in over 30 years of building Handcrafted Log Homes and 90% of the homes I built were Handcrafted. I have NEVER had any settling problems in my homes!

Nevertheless... Check with your local building inspector for any Code requirements to factor in.

Roof System Purlings and Ridge Beam

You should also plan to square up the Roof System Purlings and Ridge Beam at the point where they slip into beam pockets in the Gable ends.

This process will make it so much easier to install rafters when finishing the roof system. Just layout a square on the 2 log ends, and snap a series of lines with your chalk box for reference. Carefully chamfer and then brush down a flat area with your chainsaw, then finish the last 1/4" with a sander. This flat area will rest on the top of your framed beam in the gable beam pocket. NOTE: leave as much meat as possible! You just need a small flat surface at the bottom and (2) sides (side are optional if the log is smaller in diameter.)

NOTE: Make sure your purlins and Ridge Beam are large enough for your span requirements! Also... You should stay away from building an all log gable end if at all possible unless you plan to let the Log Shell set in your Pre-Assembly yard until it is good and dry (4-6 months). Settling issues here are much more critical than with Doors and Windows, unless you are building with Logs with a moisture content of less than 18% you should try to use a well built 2 x 6 framed gable end instead, and face it with T&G, Cedar Shingles, Log Siding or other options.

Log Siding that matches the whole logs

You can also make some Log Siding that matches the whole logs. You will need some of this when building Dormers, facing your Gable ends, or for other purposes. This can be done by starting with 2 or 3 inch thick timbers and using Makita's "Curved Planer" to carve the Natural Handcrafted Round look to the timbers.

Full-Scribe or Traditional Chinker styles of construction?

A Full-Scribe Log Home is crafted to fit together with no space at all between logs.

A Traditional Chinker Log Home is scribed at the corners only, and will have gaps of 1/2"-1-1/2" that are filled with foam backer Rod, and then chinked with a special latex material called "chinking". A number of companies supply this material, and it is designed to expand and contract up to 60% of it's original volume.

The Full-Scribe Method is a 3 step process while the Traditional Chinker requires only 2 steps. You can use a simple Saddle Notch for a traditional Chinker, but a Chamfered, Shrink-to-fit approach is better for the Full-Scribe.

There is a process called "over-scribing", that typically allows for 1/4" of settling to occur in the individual logs within the first 90 days after your Log Home is assembled. This is the period when most of the compression settling will take place. You should not worry about this if you are building a "Traditional Chinker".

If the Logs were pre-cured (air dried) to less than 18% moisture content, shrinkage of the Logs themselves will be minimal. Add this to the compression shrinkage, to be on the safe side, you will need to allow for 3-4" of total settling to occur in a 9'wall. This means that you will need to add Batt insulation over all Door & Window Header Bucks for proper sealing, then trim this with your custom Interior & Exterior door and window header trim (WIDER Than usual). (More on this in the Doors & Windows Chapter)

NOTE: All initial "major" settling should stop in a few months. (2-3 inches in usually 3-6 months) while any "compression settling" will stop in about 6-12 months, but is very little compared to the initial settling time period.

As I mentioned in an earlier chapter...I know this may seem scary to some of you ... but if done correctly, a handcrafted Log Home is awesome to live in! They are simply one of a kind. This is the only type of log home construction that can either cost you the most to build... or the least to build. This is due to the time it takes to first build the Handcrafted Log Shell, and then the time to do all of the custom fitting that is more indicitive to a Handcrafted Log Home.

If you choose to get involved in 100% of the construction process yourself... the Handcrafted Log Home can provide you with the most immediate home equity value!

Chapter 8 - Choosing the Right Logs

Throughout my career I have used many different species of Logs to build with. Some species are better than others for building a house with. Depending on where you live... the following guide will help you make the best choice.

A note about bugs in wood.

While it is true that a few bugs seem to like to chew on wood... this has been a mild issue for countless centuries of building with logs. You will simply need to spray the perimeter of your home once in a while with approved insecticides to avoid this. Bugs can be found embedded in logs after the bark is removed and will die shortly thereafter. You may find wood boring insects up in little holes after you remove the bark. If you do... simply insert an ice pick or sharp point into the hole to kill them. Much has been done in recent years to provide excellent protection against insects in wood, and it is not a big concern. It is just a part of good regular log home maintenance.

Southern Yellow Pine – A good choice, but denser and a bit harder to work with than White Pine or Lodge-pole pine. "Short Leaf" Southern Yellow Pine has the strongest tinsel strength of any conifer other than Red Fir (also known as Douglas Fir). This is why it is widely used for framing lumber today. Many homes have been built with Lodge-pole Pine and I recommend it.

Lodge-pole Pine - Mainly found in the Pacific Northwest States and is lighter, easier to use, straighter than most, and it has a great R-factor. You will want to watch the grain for any possible twisting in the grain. Don't use logs that have excessive twisting as they can open up and create challenges in the future. Many homes have been built with Lodge-pole Pine and I recommend it.

Eastern White Pine - Many consider this the best pine to use to build a home with. I agree that it typically grows straighter, it lighter colored, and is overall a strong species of Pine. Many homes have been built with Eastern White Pine and I recommend it.

Southern Red Cedar - This Cedar is also known as incense cedar and is found in many southern states and is typically used in Milled Log Homes. It generally does not grow straight enough to use as a round log unless you are using it for a character log or any other special application. This cedar like all cedars is highly resistant to decay, and makes ideal exterior log railing or porch posts. If you live in some regions of the south... this wood is the easiest and most affordable Cedar to find if you intend to build a milled log home. Many homes have been built with Southern Red Cedar and I recommend it.

Western Red Cedar - Grows in the Northern tier States. This Cedar is a great choice if you can find it or afford it. It is lighter in color than its Southern counter part, and it grows straight like pine so you can use it as whole round logs. This cedar like all cedars is highly resistant to decay, and makes ideal exterior log railing or porch posts. Many homes have been built with Western Red Cedar and I recommend it.

Tidewater Cypress - Cypress is a good choice for building with. It is very strong and resistant to decay. Grown in the Southern States it has a amber color to it. It is a little tougher to find than most woods, but one of the best choices to build with. Many homes have been built with Cypress and I recommend it.

Engelman Spruce - This is in my personal best choice to build with and has characteristics much like pine. It is a tight grained wood with good tinsel strength. Watch for twist in the grain. Many homes have been built with Engelman Spruce and I recommend it.

Alaska Spruce - is also a good choice but does not grow as straight as Engelman Spruce, and is more prone to twisting grain. Overall though it is still a good choice and has good tinsel strength. Many homes have been built with Alaska Spruce and while it is not as good a choice as other woods... I have built with it for over 7 of my 30+ years as a builder, and I recommend it. (NOTE: If you live in Alaska…Do not confuse this with "Jack Spruce", which typically grows smaller, and less durable.)

Red Fir - Grows in the Western and Northern States. It is called by more names as well. this is probably in my top 3 picks for ideal log home building material . Fir is very strong and typically grows very straight. It is also highly resistant to decay. Fir can be hard to find these days and is a bit more costly. Many homes have been built with Red Fir and I recommend it.

Hemlock - Found mostly in the western states it is hard to find large enough to build with. It also is known for twisting grain and is not a first choice to build with.

Oak – Red Oak and other Hardwoods are much harder to work with and can become almost unbearable to work with after dried. They have been used by some log home builders in milled log homes but should be avoided if possible.

Chapter 9 - Peeling Your Logs

Ah Yes... this is where we go to work.

For some this will seem to be the hardest thing they have ever done, but many a hearty lad has left their signature in every log they peel. You can peel logs in a few different ways.

Peeling Racks - First you will want to sort your logs and get them off the ground on a peeling rack. If you are using the first two methods below... you will want to get each log to about waist height. If you are using one of the last two methods... you will want the logs about 12" to 18" off the ground. Logs that will not be used in your cabin are good for this application. **NOTE: Do Not store your good logs on the ground for very long!!!!**

Using a large draw-knife - Peeling Logs with a large draw-knife is still the preferred method to get the best look. This method requires the most effort but it will yield the best results. Your approach will be to peel the bark off towards you in a rhythm that enables you to rock back on your heals with every stroke. with this method you can peel a 40' log in about 1.5 hours

Using a Curved Fence Planer - You can also use a curved fence planner made by /Makita (about $400.00) that will take much of the work out of peeling logs but you will need to master it some to get the right effect. You will be holding the back end of the tool up a bit, and rocking it into the log as you move forward with each stroke. Using this method you should be able to peel a 40' log in about 1 hour.

Here is a link to these tools: http://www.baileysonline.com/

Hydro-Peeling - You can also do what is called "Hydro-Peeling" by using a pressure washer capable of producing at least 3000 PSI with a turbo nozzle. this method strips the bark off leaving the slick surface of each log exposed. It does not give you the hewn "Handcrafted" look that a draw-knife or the curved fence planner will though. Using this method you should be able to peel a 40' log in about 30 minutes. The Pressure washer will cost about $800.00, and this method of Peeling Logs is by far the easiest and is becoming more widely used by builders as well! KEEP THE TIP MOVING!

Using a Log Wizard - Yet another method is to use what is called a "Log Wizard" chainsaw attachment. It is attached to the end of you chainsaw and is really a chainsaw powered planner. It can be dangerous to use if you do not wear chaps for protection. This method is very aggressive and will achieve the look you want if you become good with it. You should plan to use a chainsaw that is in the 25 -30 cc range. a heavier saw will quickly wear you out, and is less mobile in your hands. A Log Wizard attachment costs about $200.00 Using this method you should be able to peel a 40' log in about 30 minutes.

MILLING

Using an Alaskan Mill – An Alaskan Mill is a large chainsaw attachment that will help you mill rough cut lumber, make 3 sided D-Style logs, and cut a flat surface on a round log. The latter is important when you begin to set your base or bottom plate logs as well as Purlings, Ridge-beams, and Gable Plate Logs. A user guide comes with every Alaskan Mill, and you will get the hang of it pretty quick.

Here is a link to these tools: http://www.baileysonline.com/

Contact us with any questions regarding this process or theses tools because you will want this process to be as painless as possible. Once you have your logs peeled, most of the harder work is behind you, and you will lose some weight, and gain upper body strength in the process.

Chapter 10 - Setting Your First Logs in Place

Ok … After you have pre-qualified these previous very important issues, you are either excited to move forward or you will need to re-think your goals as it relates to building your log dream home.

If you are ready to move forward… then you will want to follow a punch list to get started. Learn to organize your information so it can be accessible to you when you need it. You should make a new punch list at least once a week, and more often as it becomes necessary. This practice will help you stay current and organized, with all phases of your Log Home construction project. Some have even kept a daily journal to keep track of all conversations and important information exchanged between Builder and Homeowner.

Below is an example of a good plan of Action:

Scenario: We will assume that You and your partner both work, and that You will be doing most of the work to start with. You will have planned to start building in March so we will assume that the following things have already been accomplished.

- *3 to 4 loads of logs purchased*
- *A Gin pole or other material handling machinery able to lift 2000 LBS. or more.*

Click here for info on Gin Poles:
http://www.logbuilding.org/GinPoles.ch5.pdf

A good Husqvarna or Sthl Chain saw between 28cc to 50cc or one of each. (you will need the small one for carving notches and the larger one for milling with).

Hand Tools

Peavy or Cant hook, a good set of scribes with bubble level attached, two or three bars, a Large Hammer, a good chisel, 4' and 2' level, chalk line, 100' and 30' tape measure, Carpenters Pencils, and Indelible Pencils, A Heavy Draw Knife to peel logs with, or a Makita Curved Fence Planer. You can have a welder make you a good Draw-Knife from some Leaf Spring stock or other hardened steel. Just Keep it Sharp with a metal wheel grinder.

You will also want to consider investing in an **Alaska Saw Mill Chainsaw Attachment.** (around $300.00 without the saw) These mills are very handy and will do most of what a larger mill will do if you know what to do with them. They just take longer.

Here is a link to these tools: http://www.baileysonline.com/

By now you will also have picked out a spot to Pre-Build the Log Shell, that is level and has plenty of room to handle the logs for a peeling area, storage of peeled and prepared logs, and of course the simulated foundation area. This will all require about 1/2 acre for a small Home or Cabin. (Be sure to think about security of your tools and building supplies in choosing this temporary pre-build site. Hopefully it will be close by where you can keep an eye on things.

NOTE: The purpose for pre-building a log shell instead of building "on-site" (your permanent foundation and sub floor) is, that building with logs can be a messy process that could scar up your building site if you try to do all that is required "on-site". It also takes a lot longer to build "on-site" even factoring in the dis-assembly and re-assembly at your building site. If you designate a "log Yard" to do this, then you would simply clean it up and back blade any disturbed soil with a CAT or Skid Steer in about 1 hour or less. The Log Shell can then be carefully inventoried, marked, labeled, and shipped to your permanent building site.

OK... The first thing that You do is layout the simulated Foundation. This should take You about 3-4 hours since you are new to this.

You start by looking at your floor plans and staking out all of your corners. On a clipboard (water proof cover) you will identify each corner in the manner that is easiest for you to orientate to your permanent build site and foundation/Sub floor. You must think in terms of two directions for each corner. To simplify this we will call these the odd course and even course direction.

The odd course is the 1st course that starts the 1/2 base or bottom Plate logs, as is pointing to the left in this photo:

NOTE: *The odd courses are the courses that are under the even courses of log wall that you are viewing left to right. The even courses are viewed head on with the log ends facing you in this photo.*

You would mill a log in two equal halves for the odd starting course. If the half log measured 5" from flat surface to crown, You would want to use an even course log that has at least 6" of flat surface and no less than 4" of wood left on the small end, after it is notched to fit over the odd course half log. Take about 1" off of your even starter log if it is about 10" to 12" in diameter to arrive where you want to be when you actually start your first course of logs. Snap a line on the starter log and begin to make long cuts in the log cutting about 2" deeper with each pass until the log is ripped into two halfs. Brush the flat surfaces with your Chainsaw to make them flat and level. Float a 2' or 4' level on your flat surfaces to find high points and carefully brush them down with your saw until they are right.

But first… let's get back to the corners. You will need a helper to hold the other end of your tape measure. Start by getting your corners laid out pretty close. Then begin to take diagonal measurements as illustrated in this drawing to verify that your corners are square. **You may need to rent a Transit or lazer level for one day to set your simulated foundation up**.

Use Large log ends about 12-15" in diameter, and stand them on end to use for your simulated temporary foundation corners. They will vary in height depending on how flat your Pre-assembly site is. You can cut a square corner on each log round with your chainsaw to simulate the corners of your foundation. Make sure the log ends are level using a 2' level to check both ways. Re-check your diagonal and square measurements for accuracy, and use some additional material to support the logs between the corners in 3-4' increments. be sure to support each side of any proposed door locations with short pieces of dunnage or scrap lumber.

When your first round of logs are in place, (both odd and even courses make one round of wall logs) then hammer a large headed roofing nail into each corner for an accurate reference point, and when you are square, trace each corner around the notches so if your logs get bumped out of place you can go back to where they need to be. Trace each corner notch of each round to give yourself a reference to go back to. Toe nail each corner together with 16 sinker framing nails.

Just continue on from here, checking your corner height from time to time to make sure your corners are within 1.5" of each other in height. in the last 2 rounds, you will "dial" this in and they will be within 1/2" of each other in overall height. Remember these are natural logs and if you do not get it absolutely perfect... Don't Sweat it!!

The Diagonals and Side measurements (See the illustration below), should be within 1/4" of each other.

Click this link for a great tool for Calculating and Squaring your foundation.

http://www.csgnetwork.com/foundationsquarecalc.html

IMPORTANT NOTE: *At each corner...you will need to Pick a point of reference at the top and crown of the log and embed a roofing nail to mark the spot. You will use these reference points later when "Re-Setting" your Log Shell on it's permanent foundation so... measure between these reference points (all diagonals & corner to corner/nail to nail) and then record them (write them down) in a notebook for future reference.*

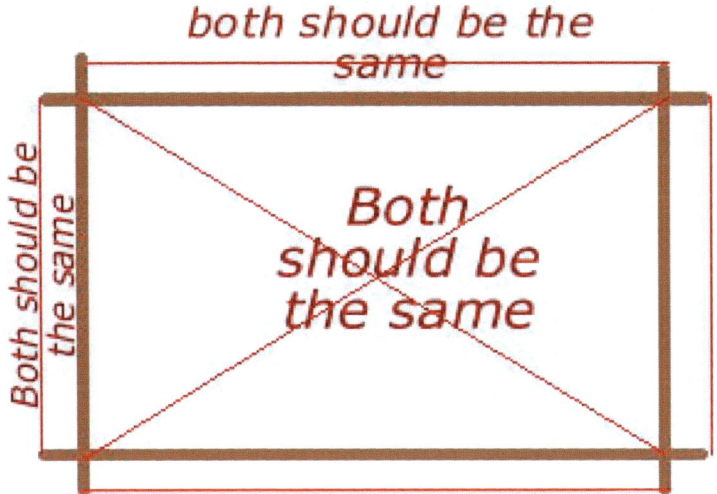

Chapter 11 – Notching Corners and Building Log Walls

Before I explain this... I want to remind you that a "ROUND" is all logs in both directions, and a "COURSE" is odd or even logs going in one or the other direction. Most Log Cabins need 12 to 13 Rounds if building with 8" minimum diameter logs to reach the height of your first roof plate log. You may want to go up another 3 or 4 rounds beyond loft height if you want to build an upper level, to obtain more usable living space in the loft area. You can also achieve this by building Large Dormers in the upper level. Less Rounds will be needed with 10" to 12" logs, or if building a Traditional Chinker style log cabin. As you begin to add logs to each Course and Round... you will want to monitor the height of each corner and select your next logs to adjust the heights at each corner. Keep in mind that corners with log butts will be a bit taller than corners with log tops. You will be alternating the tops and butts with each course and round, so they will average out to be about the same as you notch each round of logs in place. Try to stay within 2 inches at all times as this will help you fine tune in the top two rounds as well as keep your walls looking uniform. When you get to the round or course that will be your "Cap" logs over doors and windows... try to use logs slightly larger for added strength. If you plan to go up at least 3 courses higher than your door and window heights... this won't matter as much. Most of the time it is much easier to build the walls without cutting door and window rough openings out, and just cut them on-site after the log shell has been re-assembled on the permanent Sub-floor and Foundation. The logs are much easier to handle especially when you are new to this process.

However... I strongly advise that you consider cutting the flat surface or header area in the logs that cap over your doors and windows, because if you don't... eventually you will be trying to cut them upside down and this requires some experience to pull off with out making mistakes. So when you get to the Cap logs, just measure and draw reference lines with a level while the log is up on the wall in place. Then take it off the wall and cut your top flat surfaces down on the same horses you are using to notch your corners with. Just draw a level line on the end of the logs while they are still up on the wall. Then when on the ground... turn the log while using the level at the end of the log. This will get your flat spot very level and save you a ton of headache! Now just cut out the bulk of the wood and brush the header area down to your lines with your saw, and finally the last details can be cleaned up with a small 4" sander/Grinder with a 36 grit flexible round sanding disc. Use your level to make sure your header surface is level, and check your lines on the end of the log to make sure they stay plumb or level throughout his process.

Notching

This process starts by selecting a log for the wall you are working on. Hoist it on top of the wall and resting on the (2) logs ends that it will be scribed over. When lined up on the wall correctly... begin by calibrating your scribes, and setting them to about 1" less than what would be touching the log below or to the spot that is the most narrow between the the log you are scribing and the log below. Keep the scribes cocked at about 35 degrees, but perfectly plumb and then starting at the lowest point, bring the scribes up slowly, and smoothly, to mark or "scribe" the notch. Do this for each side. NOTE: The small end should be scribed with at least ½" less of a mark than the "Butt" end. This is so the remain somewhat level as the wall is built. Any other additional height that is needed will come with the next log as you alternate ends.

If you do this right... you will never take out more than 2/3 of the diameter of each log after the notch is finished. There are exceptions to this but try to target ½ if the log's diameter as the finished notch. If you scribe less than half... you will experience what is called "Re-Curve", and this is when you leave too much and the next log cannot scribe and notch over the log below, without making larger gaps in the sides of the notches where the crown of the log below "breaks Over". If you practice first on a smaller single corner demo project... you will get a sense of how to get this right within 3 to 4 rounds.

Each time you scribe a notch, you may need to darken the line to see it better before carving it out with your saw. Keep the line thin, and use indelible ink pencils so that when you mist spray with water, the line will show up better. Fire up your chain saw, put on some safety glasses, and begin to cut slices down to within 1 inch of your scribe line. Your slices should be about an inch wide or less so you can knock them away with a hammer. After you have taken most of the wood out of the way, you can wiggle the tip of your bar at medium RPMs to begin to fine tune the shape or "bowl of the notch. DON'T GO TOO DEEP!... this will weaken the notch. Just get most of the wood out of the way and turn off your saw for now.

Then get your heavy duty ¾ inch wood chisel and begin to cut or chisel down about 1/2 inch below the line. Start by placing the beveled surface of the chisel towards the inside of the notch, and strike the chisel 3 or 4 times until you have reached a depth of ½ inch. Try to flick the excess wood away. This process will be repeated around the entire scribe line of the notch, so that when you return to using the saw to clean out the remaining wood... the edge at the scribe line will not be buggered and chipped out by your chainsaw. Last details around the edge of the notch can be cleaned up with a small 4" sander/Grinder with a 36 grit flexible round sanding disc. Another great tool is called a "Sharkie", but they are dangerous if not used properly. The Goal is to leave a notch in such a way that if you took a piece of flat metal and ran it around the scribe line... it would touch nothing but the sharp wood edge of the notch. Look at the log it will notch over, and look for any wood bulges, knots or other areas that would hit the inside of the notch and hold the log up. Simply chisel or "brush these areas down" with your chainsaw so that your notch will come down and fit tight over the log below!

Just take your time scribing your notches, and you will get great results!

Chapter 12 - Laying Out and Building Your Loft

If you choose to include a loft in your floor-plan... you will give yourself additional living space at very little extra cost due to the fact that "building up" eliminates additional roof build-up and foundation/flooring costs. You may need to use flat or pitched dormers to utilize more usable space... but even these costs are less than additional roof buildup and foundation/flooring costs.

So... you will need to think in terms of installing log floor joists on 3' – 4' on centers. Your log floor joists will be installed after you have reached a log wall height of at least 9' on the long sides of your home. You will then choose the right number of logs at least 9" in diameter, and mill a 1/2" to 1" thick flat spot on the log. This should give you just enough of a flat surface to lay out your flooring system. These logs should be as straight as possible and very similar in size. After you have milled your flat surface on each one... Climb up on your ladder and mark out your layout on top of both opposite walls. load all of your log floor joists on to the walls, with the bottom round crown area positioned on top of each layout mark. (you will need to extend your layout mark down over the wall log about 6" to 8" to be able to see it and line up the logs later when re- positioning them). Then using a 2' level... make sure that all of the log floor joists are perfectly level, and carefully chock or set them firmly in place with rocks, not wood chips as they will break and spin or rotate the log out of place.

Now you will set-up your transit level on one corner using a triangular piece of 3/4" plywood as a temporary platform. (Be careful as you are now 9' to 10' in the air looking through the transit scope.) with a helper... find the measurement of each floor joist at each point that you will be cutting a notch in the floor joist. Unlike wall logs where you can take out up to ½ of the log diameter for your notch... in the case of log floor joists you do not want to notch any more than 1/3 of the log's diameter to avoid weakening the notch. You will need to do a "cutback" of the "Re-Curve" to avoid gaps in the lower portion of the notch. If you want to skip this step... simply be prepared to chink the notches to fill in those gaps. These gaps occur due to the fact that since you are not taking out much of the notch... the log surface will curl under and the next notch will leave a gap.

After you have captured the measurement for each notching point (from the flat spot to the cross hair of the transit scope using a survey stick or rigid tape measure), simply find the lowest measurement (the longest measurement), and the highest measurement (the shortest measurement). These should be within 1-1/2" of each other if you picked logs the same size. Alternating the tops and butts will be the best idea. Simply choose the minimum notch size for the shortest one, and bring every other notch or flat surface measurement to match that one. Then scribe each notch with each individual notch size required to arrive with all flat surfaces the same. Scribe both sides just like a corner notch, with an indelible pencil. When all notches are scribed... you can either notch the logs up on the building, or take them down in order with your tractor or Skid steer, and begin to carefully notch them. MAKE SURE YOU DON'T OVER CUT YOUR NOTCHES.

After the notches are all carved out... put them back up in place and re-measure your flat surfaces at the point of the notch. If they are off a bit...begin to fine tune.

When all of your floor joists are in place... you can select some additional wall logs to cap over all of the log floor joists. You will be doing a bunch more notches, but after these logs are in place, you will need one or two more rounds to complete the log walls. The last log on the long side (usually the odd course), will have a flat surface milled into it, and will be placed on the wall turning it to match the pitch of your roof line. A 12/12 pitch is easiest to calculate and will give you a bit more head room in the loft area, but is quite steep and you will need to keep this in mind when installing your roofing components.

NOTE: For any logs that span over walkways, archways, or common areas in general... Most Codes require a minimum pass thru height of at least 6'-8" or 80" Bear this in mind as you calculate for loft logs, Girders, and Settling allowances.

<u>Check with your local building inspector for any Code requirements to factor in.</u>

Loft Flooring

Your flooring system can either be 2x6 Tongue & Groove then 3/4" sub-flooring, or you can install a sleeper floor system.

The first alternative is the simplest method, but you will need to pre-plan your plumbing and wiring as you will not be able to route any of this using this method.

With the "Sleeper System" you would install 1x6" or 1x8" Tongue & Groove over the log joists for looks (remember... this is the material you will look up and see every day). Then just use either 2x4 or 2x6 floor joists 16" on center with 3/4" sheets of sub-flooring over that. Remember to consult with your HVAC system installer, for any ducting to install in between the framed floor joists as well as wiring, plumbing drain, phone, data lines, or other elements before laying down your 3/4" sub-flooring. Remember... Water Plumbing and Electrical lines do not mix!

Typical look of a log floor joist system

Chapter 13 - Proper Roof Design

Many years ago we were asked to tour and do a restoration audit on a 300 acre Resort with over 130 Handcrafted log structures on it. One of the main things we found was that the roof design on most of the buildings, Lodges, and Cabins were designed with only 14" to 18" of Gable and eve overhang.

While this is common for "Stick-Built" Homes, it is a serious "No-No" for Log Structures. This is because even if it is Kiln-Dried Log Siding or Handcrafted Whole logs, they all will have some checking. Checking is the random cracks found throughout a log or siding product. It is a natural process for wood to open up a little after it has been cut down. With checking then you run a greater risk of moisture infiltration. Also...Logs will naturally de-hydrate and re-hydrate and will never lose all of their moisture. So it is important to provide protection from the natural elements, in your overall roof overhang design. This will prevent unnecessary damage from the elements.

Minimizing Checking

A Great way to minimize checking is by cutting in a "Drying Kerf" on the top crown of the log the full length of the logs ...to force the log to open at that line. This is a good idea and we made a practice of doing it on both the top and bottom of each log used in a handcrafted Log home. With a "Full Scribe" home... the under V groove will suffice for the bottom of the log.

If building a "Traditional Chinker"...you simply snap a line down most of the length of the log on the top an bottom, and cut a chainsaw kerf about 1" deep. This will help minimize checking, but some checking will still occur, and is a natural part of building with Logs.

You will want to be very careful about designing your Log home for good protection at the eves and gable ends. Without at least 3 feet of gable end overhang, and 2 feet of eve overhang, you will risk unwanted exposure to the elements. Conventional built homes generally don't use a translucent finish and may not need this protection. Log Structures do... so design lots of overhang into your roof system. It looks better as well!

Also... I recommend that you use the strongest and simplest Log Roof Support System on your Home or Cabin... The Post and Beam, or "Purling System". Porches are also a great way to protect your log walls but they of course will ad some additional expense to your building budget.

Another Roof design tip is to try to plan for the design of a 6/12 to 9/12 roof pitch for your Home. This covers both aesthetic appeal and Snow Load issues if you live in a Northern Colder Region. If you build with any steeper pitch, and plan to have a Roofing Professional Roof your home... they will charge you more to cover the time it takes to apply extra safety measures.

<u>Check with your local building inspector for any Code requirements to factor in.</u>

Roof insulation

We have used Fiberglass Batts up to 12" thick in Alaska, and we have used polyurethane foam which generally is rated at 7.2 R-factor per inch. Your will need at least an R-38 rating in your roof to keep your Heating and Cooling Costs down. There is a 10" Fiberglass Batt Insulation available as well. It is called "condensed", and has a rating of R-38.

You will also want to plan for a minimum of an R-19 rating in your Log Walls. University Studies conducted many years ago in Canada and the US determined that an 8" Pine Log would provide an R-19 rating for your walls. This is why so many 6" milled Log Products were covered up with interior stud walls after being built. The rule of thumb for this again is applied in terms of "Thermal Mass"heating and cooling. The Larger the Log Structure the bigger the Logs it will require.

Thermal Mass is how a solid material heats and cools. While a "Stick-Built Home" will heat up from a cold temperature much faster, it will also fluctuate throughout the day and your HVAC System will cycle on and off more often.

A Log Structure may take several hours to thoroughly heat up... but it will maintain it's temperature much better through Thermal Mass. The same principals apply to Summer cooling as well.

Check with your local building inspector for any Code requirements to factor in.

Girders and Spanning

When designing a girder or Log Beam for support, a 12" Minimum is the general rule of thumb, and you will not want to span over 20 feet with a load bearing log of less than 12" in diameter unless supported by a vertical log or supporting wall with 2x6"studs compiled to 9" thick.

Examples:

- A 11" load bearing log can only free span 17' without support.

- A 12" load bearing log can only free span 20' without support.

- A 13" load bearing log can only free span 23' without support.

Add 1" of horizontal Log diameter required to span for each additional 3 ' over the 20' distance without using a vertical Log used to support it. There is a Span Table Booklet available that has been the standard reference guide for both Canada and the US since the 1960's get it here: http://www.loghomestore.com

Check with your local building inspector for any Code requirements to factor in.

To view the anatomy of a log home and the "Purling Roof Support System" click on this link: the Isometric Drawing link on our Web site:
http://www.theloghomeguide.com/isometric_drawing.html

Check with your local building inspector for any Code requirements to factor in.

In this photo... This is a Log Roof Support System on a Hybrid or System-Built Log Home with framed walls and Handcrafted log Siding.

Chapter 14 - Building Your Roof System

There are a few different methods of building a log cabin roof system, but the easiest is the "Post & Beam" method.

The pictures below will illustrate some of what I am about to tell you.

The best way to build your roof system is to simply frame up the gable ends with slots for the squared point at which the log will slide down into the beam pocket as illustrated here. These beam pockets will have a framed post using 2x6 dimensional lumber and screwed together to make a post from 9" to 12" wide. You would then use OSB to sheet over the framed gable end. Use construction adhesive and maybe screws for this as well!

To find the points at which you will build beam pockets, you will need to use some graph paper to determine the roof pitch. It would be better to make your framed beams or posts about 2" shorter than you calculate, to avoid having to modify them and cut them down when already in place. This is also illustrated in the "ISOMETRIC DRAWING" on our site.) By making them shorter... you may just need to shim up a bit to arrive at the perfect pitch plane. All of the Purlings, and the Ridge Beam... should have a flat surface milled on them similar to the log floor joists, except at the exact pitch of the roof system. Your 2x12 rafters will plane vertically and rest on the purlings and Ridge Beam, and your 5/8" OSB Roof Sheathing will glue and nail to them. This will give your roof system the strength it needs.

You will need to practice a couple of times on disposable short logs to get the concept of squaring a round log at the ends, and at any point between the ends. It simply involves using a level, and speed square to make sure you are doing the same thing on both ends. You will also need to factor in the pitch of the roof and use a couple of stout saw horses with a slight v notch cut in so you will be able to spin the log to the right pitch before your begin to layout the squared areas. Use a chalk line to snap along the length of the log to keep all of your calculations and measurements accurate. Then using your carving saw... gently cut the starting curve and then begin to flatten out your cut about ½ " above where your finish surface is to be. Then simply "Brush Down" the wood to within 1/4", and then sand it down with a sander/grinder to the finish surface from there.

You can also add a log truss (as pictured below here) to your roof design for looks and support.

When you are ready to install your framed gable ends...you will want to be prepared to brace all of this off with 2x6 braces and cross bracing as much as possible. You or your roofing crew will be climbing around on this until it becomes rigid and without danger of collapsing, so don't get careless at this point. Strong winds are very destructive as well so until you have your roof build up finished... KEEP IT BRACED GOOD!

Build A Model!

Another great way to understand how to build your log cabin including the roof support system... is to build a model of your log cabin first! This can be done with dowels, a router, and a small hobby band or scrolling saw to cut miniature lumber. Try to scale it with the logs as 1" dowels that way your wall logs will be 12" in diameter in scale. You can use ¾ for 8" logs posts etc., and 7/8" dowels for roof support logs.

The illustration scale model below is an example of a "Butt and Pass" Log Cabin. It is showing additional Log Rafters over the Purlings, and Ridge Beam which are not necessary, but will provide a surface structure for your 3/4" Tongue & Groove Pine or Cedar to nail to.

Check with your local building inspector for any Code requirements to factor in.

Chapter 15 - All about Windows and Doors

Windows

Like finishes... Windows and Doors are an extremely important issue with a Log Home. By nature the design of most Log Homes require more windows to bring in added light to brighten up each room. This is also lends itself to giving you more of what you want to see near your building site...generally a great view of nature. But there are more things to consider when it pertains to windows.

The term "Nomenclature" is used to describe how components such as windows are designed for proper placement, positioning, and sizing. There are basically 5 types of windows. All Vinyl, Vinyl Clad Wood, Aluminum Clad Wood, All Aluminum, and All Wood.

We also know that more windows will mean more potential cost in heating and cooling, so you want a good quality window. You could buy discount windows but you will definitely pay the difference eventually... many times over if you don't get good ones.

Vinyl Windows:

- Nearly 80% of all windows sold in the U.S. are vinyl windows.

- Of that 80% over 62% are sold by The Home Depot. (The reason for this is that they have an agreement with Anderson Windows/ American Craftsman)

- And of that 62% nearly 86% are American Craftsman Vinyl Windows.

American Craftsman or (Silverline to some) is owned by Anderson Doors and windows. I have used these windows and can boldly recommend that if you use Vinyl Windows... Use American Craftsman by Anderson. (BTW…I did not get paid to endorse them or make this statement.)

I have also been to numerous seminars and trade shows, featuring many window manufacturers and after all these years... I still am fond of the Anderson brand of Windows. Other good windows are Eagle, Pella, Hurd, Peachtree, Marvin, Phillips-Marquee(vinyl), Jeld-wen Caradco, Lincoln and a few others.

When considering what you want in a window, you need to include a strong consideration of Low-E glass.

Low-E glass was reportedly first designed in WW2 for Airplane cockpits to reduce cabin temperatures, and glare. It was reported to reduce fatigue during long bombing missions, and keep the cabin cockpit cooler. Low-E is a small additional investment in each window's cost. (about 8-12%). It is a minimum requirement in some states now and in the last 15 years I never used anything else in the homes I built.

All Aluminum Windows will Transfer Heat and Cold 70% faster than Wood, Clad Wood, or Vinyl. They are inexpensive, but should be avoided anywhere North of the Mason-Dixon Line.

Vinyl Clad Wood Windows are a great choice, especially for a Log Home because you will have the Vinyl exposed to the elements, and natural wood to the inside.

All Wood Windows should be avoided unless you are restoring a historical building or simply want the all wood look. Jeld-Wen makes the best all wood window in my opinion. They are made of wood sash frames that are treated throughout the entire wood components, and are processed to penetrate 96% of the wood fiber. Home Depot or Lowe's carry the best all-around selection of quality doors and windows for the price. Go into your local Home Depot or Lowe's, and speak to their mill work specialist to get an idea of what your window budget should be.

About Doors

There are basically 4 types of Exterior entry doors:

- **Metal primed skin over ridged foam**
- **Fiberglass skinned doors with composite wood inside**
- **Vinyl or aluminum Clad over solid wood interior**
- **Solid wood doors**

Fiberglass Doors come either smooth, or with a molded wood look-a-like texture. The benefit of fiberglass is that it won't stick to your door jamb when it gets humid outside. It is also very durable material. fiberglass doors are also a bit spendy. I recommend Feather River Fiberglass Doors, or Pella.

Metal Skinned Doors are less costly, but will need to be painted a color that will go well with your Log home. I recommend Jeld-wen metal doors. They offer some very nice glass options and are well built.

Vinyl or Aluminum Clad over Wood Patio Doors, are used very often in new Log Homes. These Doors are beautiful, but once again a bit costly. I recommend Anderson for this kind of door. They are well designed and have a great warranty.

Solid Wood Doors - Last but not least is the beautiful, cost effective, solid Fir, Oak, Yellow Pine, or Mahogany wood Door. This is a good choice if... You apply the right finishes correctly, and if your door is protected by a porch or other entry that is not exposed to direct sunlight. So... the ideal door in my opinion for a Log Home, is a Solid Wood door, that has a very good finish of exterior grade oil-based finishes, that are applied to **ALL SIX DOOR SURFACES**!! Yep... 6 sides or surfaces! You must apply finishes to all-wood exterior doors so that the top, bottom (especially the bottom), hinge side, lock side, front and back are protected. You do not want a drop of moisture to find its way into the wood. Wood naturally de-hydrates, and re-hydrates, so you must not allow it to do this or you will have problems with your door sticking to the jamb in humid weather. Just seal it well with a high quality finish, and you will enjoy the beauty of a natural solid wood entry door.

I recommend you do your homework and choose the company who has a solid wood door right for your log home. Some companies will make you a custom carved entry door.

Make sure you or your builder knows the proper way to install doors and windows. **NEVER USE HIGH EXPANDING SPRAY FOAM WITH DOORS AND WINDOWS**. Use a soft cure, minimal expanding foam if you need to. If you don't you will put unnecessary pressure on your doors and windows, and could have problems with their operation.

NOTE: Using High Expanding Spray Foam will also void the warranty on your doors and windows with most manufacturers. Just use the soft cure foam and good common sense in properly sealing out any weather or air infiltration.

Check with your local building inspector for any Code requirements to factor in.

Chapter 16 - Milled Log Home Options

Milled Log Homes Milled Log homes are a great option to the more expensive handcrafted Log home if your are employing a builder. One important key is to use logs large enough to avoid furring out the inside to get a good R-Factor. A Good seal between the Logs is very important with any log Home, but especially true with smaller Logs. (6-8"). Smaller milled logs can twist and lift, causing brakes in the seal between the Logs. Try to choose a milled log home Supplier who offers a multiple spleen Tongue and Groove system. One of the best systems for maintaining a good seal between the Logs is a system that employs a combination of all thread to join the first (4) courses, then Timber Screws for all courses after that.

Some additional questions to ask your potential Milled log home Supplier are:

1. Do the Logs come in lengths shorter than 8' ? - As a rule they should not! Too many small lengths of Logs tend to look chopped up, so try to use longer lengths on longer walls.

2. What is the moisture content of the Logs? - Many will try to sell you on their "kiln-Dried" Logs. Wood exposed to the elements naturally hydrates, and de-hydrates with the seasons, and Logs are no different. Even a "kiln-Dried" Log will always retain 8 - 12% moisture when in the elements. Even if you seal it well some moisture will find it's way in. This is just fine, because a little bit of moisture in your logs won't hurt anything. Logs need to breath to hydrate, and de-hydrate with the seasons.

NOTE: You will be tempted to not allow for settling with a milled log home, but unless it is Cypress, or Cedar, (which exchange moisture much less after curing), then allow at least 1" for overall settling.

3. Do they sell the logs by the lineal foot or as a package price? You will want to compare prices for both of these buying options before you decide.

Most are asking approx. $6.00 to $8.00 per lineal foot for "Kiln Dried" Logs that measure 6"-8" as a D-Style .

4. What does the surface of their milled log look like? - Some milled Log home suppliers produce logs that can have a rough, stringy look. You are paying for this, so ask them to send you a sample log of what your logs will look like when shipped to you as a package. Some of this can easily be cleaned up, but you should see a consistent quality close to your sample in the end.

If you can find the logs from a smaller company that has not yet franchised or is offering Logs at $4.00 per lineal foot or less...you may want to seriously consider this option.

Below is an example of a Milled Log Home:

<u>**Check with your local building inspector for any Code requirements to factor in.**</u>

Chapter 17 - TheAdvanced Handcrafted or Hybrid Log Home

Hybrid Log Homes are the newest trend to the Log Home Industry. They are best described as a combination of "Conventional Stick Frame", and solid log accents. Typically the home will be 2x6 framing and exterior Log Siding. This Log Siding can be a simple milled 6", 8" or wider, and about 1 1/2" thick. Or it can also be siding that has been processed to look handcrafted, in up to 14" widths and up to 4" thick in the center.

This style is becoming more and more popular because it creates many more options to the buyer. With a stick frame insulated core, the interior is open to many more options in wall finishes. You can use all drywall, with just a few Log accents, or you can use all Log siding on the inside walls, or a combination of both. There are even methods to use full log Roof Support beams in a Hybrid Log Home.

Many times these Log Homes are called "System-built", or "Panelized" Log Homes and can be purchased in complete packages with all wall sections pre-built. These packages will come with all exterior Log Siding applied to the wall sections, Finishes pre-applied, and all windows pre-installed with exterior window trim of your choice.

These Log Homes can be expensive so do your homework! When these Log Home Packages are delivered to your home site, you will need a crane to lift and place each wall section where it belongs in your floor plan. These packages are designed to go together in a short amount of time, and can be dried-in in as little as 1 week, with all interior work ready to be completed. Another benefit to this method is that there is no settling to worry about. This method is also user friendly to many "Stick Frame" builders because it is built with most of the methods already familiar to these builders.

You can build the wall using this approach and make you own unique log siding using the curved fence planer, or a "Log Wizard" chainsaw attachment.

Below are photos of (2) System-Built/ Hybrid Log Homes under construction.

Check with your local building inspector for any Code requirements to factor in.

Chapter 18 - Choosing the Right Log Home Supplier

In my 30+ years as a Log Home student and builder, I have seen many log Home companies come and go. But there are many who have continued the tradition of supplying quality products to their customers. I have used many of their products, but in the interest of fairness, I will simply supply you with links, testimonials, and forums to help you make up your own mind who to do business with.

If you purchase my personal consulting services... I will be more specific on this matter.

Below… I have compiled a basic but accurate rating system that may help you in the decision making process.

I will give you my opinion on what I think a good log home Supplier should provide you to earn a rating of 5 on a scale from 1-5… 5 being the highest in value.

Customer Support

If they are prompt in returning phone calls & emails, reply to their own inquiry forms promptly, and are willing to interact with you consistently; but without a high pressure approach… they should be near the 4-5 points range. Most good Log Home suppliers will make available to you a phone and email contact for support when you get ready to build. Some will send free of charge a tech for the first 1-3 days. If they are willing to send a factory Rep to you for a day or two, to make sure the first few courses are right … they merit high marks…..4-5 points.

NOTE: Many Handcrafted Log Home Companies will insist on setting the first course of logs on your foundation sub-floor, to insure that it is installed exactly as it was in their pre-assembly yard. If this is not done right, each course of Logs will continue to show fit variances as it goes together on your site. Each log is marked in the Pre-assembly process, to go back together just as it was pre-crafted in the Log Yard. *On the other* hand... if you decide to do this yourself... just request a first round layout sheet with exact measurements indicated on it from point to point, and just keep fussing with the first round until it is on your sub-floor exactly as described by the kit supplier's measurements. When you are confident that it is right on... nail and screw the first round down with nails and timber screws. Just be careful to line up the rest of the log shell perfectly from here on up to the last log.

Complete Package or options?

If they offer a variety of options at reasonable prices… 4-5 points (you will need to compare for the best evaluation of this) Some Log Home suppliers will try to sell you the complete package. If you can, separate the Log package from the add-ons that they offer, and price these from your local building supply. These add-ons may cost much more in shipping, and can be purchased usually for less at your local building supply. They may raise the cost of just the log package without your purchase of the complete package, so do the math!

Shipping Costs

If they are close to trucking Industry Rates… 4 – 5 points Shipping costs are getting higher and higher with the cost of fuel rising. These costs will vary from week to week but a few phone calls to flatbed freight carriers, should give you some accurate info. They charge you by the loaded mile and for fuel surcharges. Currently these rates are between $2.25 - 2.75 per loaded mile from the point of origin.

Warranties of 10 years or more

4-5 points. Most good Log Home suppliers will give you a conditional warranty of at least 10 years or more. These conditions will vary and relate to your commitment to do scheduled preventative maintenance on your Log

Home, as well as the experience level of the builder you choose to build or assemble their product. Ask each supplier for that information.

Builder Friendly Assembly

If you & your builder are comfortable with this process, then the supplier has provided you with good information and support…4-5 points Make sure that the Log Home supplier provides several copies of good blue prints, and that the assembly instructions are user friendly. This can be a real help when you or your builder get lost, even if they provide great customer support! ….4-5 points

Other things that are a plus are:

An information overview for your lender describing what you get for your money and the estimated time it may take to Dry-in the Log Home package. This is information that your lender may require to close the Construction loan and get you on your way.

A brief phone conference with you, the Log Home supplier, your Builder, and your Lender just prior to closing your construction loan, and getting started.

A few references from customers of your Log Home supplier. Most will be happy to supply this information.

A delivery date commitment from your Supplier. This can be very important if you have made arrangements for your builder and his crew to start when your Log Home package is delivered.

Choosing the right Builder

If you decide you don't want to save a ton of money and build a Log Home or Vacation Cabin yourself... then this is probably one of the most important choices you will make. If at all possible don't let money influence your decision-making!!!

I can't stress this enough!

You will get what you pay for unless you are lucky to find an experienced builder who needs the work at that time, and is willing to compete with the less experienced "up-starts". I was once an upstart, and made some mistakes along the way, but the difference is in the integrity of any builder who will stand behind his work. Treat your builder with respect, communicate with him, and he will work hard for you. You will save time and money in the long run if you choose a builder who has a good reputation for quality work. There is a reason for this. He has recruited a good crew made up of dependable workers who will be consistent both in quality, and commitment to their employer. There is added value in paying a little extra for "the Right Stuff". Get acquainted with your builder and make sure he submits a copy of his credentials to you as well as some recent references. Check with his suppliers to get a sense of his character.

There are some very good builders out there who stay very busy for a reason. It may be worth it to be put on a waiting list for your project. Let's pause our qualifying exercise for a moment, and consider some additional variables that you will want to bear in mind. If you choose to employ a Builder…no matter how little you know about construction, or how little time you have to be at your log home construction site… you will need to have a good communication with your builder. You must trust him to stay within your budget, and do quality work at the same time. Communication with your Builder is a must, if you want to maintain quality control, and stay on budget! ...

OK……. pause here and ponder what we've just covered, grab a cup of coffee, and relax…. I know you were tensing up when we covered "communication with your builder", but believe me there are some great builders out there that will want to make you a happy, proud Log Home owner, and who value your referral to future potential customers. So as long as You and your Builder are clearly on the same page, you should see great results from him.

Chapter 19 - Log Home Finishes

This topic has been the discussion of many suppliers and builders in the Log Home Industry over the years. While there are many excellent companies who manufacture log home finishes, there are some proven products that have withstood the test of time, and are recommended by us.

These are the attributes of good Log Home finishes:

Rule # 1.

Use Oil-based products not latex products!

The original Log Home Finishes, going back several decades contained natural linseed oil that penetrated into the log wood fibers, which resulted in several layers of protection. While offering superior protection from the elements when applied correctly as needed, these finishes caused the logs to turn dark, and looked less desirable.

So... in the 1980's several companies started producing latex water based products. These products were designed for the "Lazy Log Home Owner", because they laid on top of the log wood fibers like a latex glove, and required less of a maintenance effort initially. The trouble with this approach is that it gave the homeowner a false sense of security, and more often created lazy, bad habits such as not properly preparing the Log Home's surface between additional coats. This would result in costly problems years down the road.

Latex finishes were beautiful for a few short years then would peel like a bad sunburn. Although these products are still offered today... the pendulum is once again swinging back to oil and paraffin-based log home finishes.

The Oil-based finishes do require some initial commitment from the homeowner to acquire a penetrating base of protection over the first few years, but this commitment is by far the best investment you will ever make in the long-term integrity of your Log Home's Exterior.

Don't be lazy!... with a high quality Garden Sprayer and the right finishes you can maintain the beauty of your Log Home for years to come!

Here is the rule of thumb for new construction or recent restoration when it comes to protecting a Log Home's Exterior:

<u>Year 1</u> - at least 2 coats maybe 3 if the Logs are very dry. These coats will protect your log home better if you stay away from an airless sprayer, and use a good quality Garden Sprayer to apply the finishes.

WAIT!... YOU MUST BACK BRUSH THE FINISH WITH A LARGE BRUSH TO GET IT TO PENETRATE INTO THE WOOD FIBERS. DON'T MAKE THE MISTAKE OF SKIPPING THIS IMPORTANT STEP. You can use a long broom handle with the brush to make this task easier.

<u>Year 2</u> - 1 coat …you will want to do a water test in early spring on the logs. Especially the first 4 courses to see how well the finish is holding up. Again... if your logs are really dry, you may need more.

NOTE: Initially you will need to determine the color of the finish you want to use. Bear in mind that the UV rays of the sun will turn your logs gray or worse if you don't use at least a light color pigment in your finish. As you add coats this will add more color and a deeper hue to your logs.

<u>Year 3</u> - You should be able to skip this year, but do the water test to see if the water beads on the first 4 courses. If it does not... you will at least need to apply more finish to those areas.

<u>Year 4</u> - Apply finishes as needed, and from here on out just keep an eye on your investment!. Do a water test from time to time with a misting squirt bottle to assess your protection. So… Whether you choose to use latex or Oil-based log Home Finishes, do yourself a huge favor, and…

***DO IT RIGHT!!* You'll be satisfied when you go the extra mile to complete a task the right way. Here are some great links to Log Home Finishes and information:**

http://www.logfinish.com/
http://www.loghelp.com/
http://www.loghomestore.com/sc23-finishes.php
http://www.messmers.com/
http://www.logassociation.org/directory/stains_sealants.php
http://www.penofin.com/products_logon.shtml

Chapter 20 - HVAC Heating and Cooling Systems

Important Fact!: There are (4) major components that are the most important in a log Home or Cabin to get maximum energy efficiency.

Note: these are not necessarily in the order of priority or importance

The HVAC Design in your home
The "Low - E" factor in Windows
The overall size of the Logs you are using
Caulking and Sealing your roof line, Doors, Windows, and your   Logs.
(the most overlooked but very important.)

We will now cover the HVAC Design in your home.

HVAC stands for: Heating, Ventilating, and Air Conditioning...This is a very important part of your Log Home's pre-construction planning. Spend the time to get 2 or 3 quotes on what would be the best system for your floor plan. Make sure you explain in great detail how your home is laid out, and let your HVAC Tech. look at your floor plan before he provides you with an estimate.

Log Cabins by design are often more "open" floor plans than conventional homes, so the delicate balance of heating and cooling all areas equally is very important. Having your return ducts in the right location is very important, as well as choosing a system that will not cycle on and off constantly, thus creating higher heating and cooling costs for you in the long run. Fans and their location are a must to plan well in an open floor plan.

Another consideration is to install a system with a multiple speed air handling capability. Spending a little more for the right system, is a priority investment that will pay you back in the future. Consult with a good tech in your area for what the proper system should be for your log home… then get a couple more opinions on the matter. This is extremely important! If at all possible install a Heat Pump System, with either a wood stove or fireplace to help in the winter. In the winter time depending on where you live... a heat pump may not be able to heat enough below 20 degrees Fahrenheit. Talk with your HVAC Tech in your area for more on this. For the most part you will need 1 ton of heating capacity in your system for every 350 to 450 SQ. FT. for a Log Home. The Cooling side of your system is rated in "Seer", and again you will want to get a 12 to 14 seer system to cover your cooling needs. You will also need to understand how your HVAC System is rated in terms of "Tons". Without going into a lot of techie stuff, it is safe to assume that you will want to have your system rated at 3 tons or higher. Many larger homes need up to a 6 ton system.

The new high efficiency standard for today's new construction also uses a multi-Speed Air handling unit. This is designed to only move the air that you need at certain times of the day, in certain rooms. This way you are not consuming more energy than you actually need to condition the air efficiently in all areas of your home.

For smaller Cabins I would also like to encourage you to look into the new trend in HVAC called the Ductless Heat Pump.

http://goingductless.com/consumer/about-ductless-heating-and-cooling

http://www.ezinearticles.com/?Understanding-a-Ductless-Heat-Pump

One other great break through in electric heat is led by a company called EdenPure, and they feature the EdenPure Quartz Infrared Portable Heater. The EdenPure TM uses a new advanced quartz infrared heating system that never reaches a temperature that can start a fire, and they look great as well. These appliances are best suited for a small cabin.

http://www.edenpurestore.com/

There are so many choices out there and it really depends on where you live as to what will work best for you, so get in touch with your local HVAC Professionals to help you make a wise decision on your HVAC System. **Check with your local building inspector for any Code requirements to factor in.**

Chapter 21 – Log Cabin Interior Design

This is an area that we will mostly leave to your tastes and lifestyle. But there are some things to consider when it comes to Interior design.

In General your interior decor and design should be somewhat "Rustic" or a combination of rustic and other more common design elements you want to be included.

The allure of a Log Home or Vacation Cabin is the extremely relaxing atmosphere you enjoy living in the country, or at least closer to nature. This is then perhaps the way you should measure your tastes for what you want to include in your interior design.

Many people have struggled with leaving some of the second floor "open to below". If you are building a Log Home to accommodate a large family then this may be important to you. But if you do build with a full loft or second floor... you may not enjoy one of the most relaxing and comfortable aspects of living in a Log Home. That is the open lofty feeling of the vaulted ceiling and the exposed Log roof support system. An open design in a smaller cabin is easier to heat and cool as well.

If you are building a small log home or cabin, just leaving a quarter section of your second floor living area "open to below", will make a big difference in the atmosphere of your home.

When it comes to interior walls, don't be afraid to include some drywall in your partition walls, or other wood accents other than just Logs. This will serve to make your Log Walls "Pop" or your other walls against the backdrop of your log walls "Pop" as well, if that is your desire.

When you have decided on what you want... Make it your own... it will be your Log Home Lifestyle, and environment for years to come!

Chapter 22 - A Rock Fireplace for under $1000

I know this sounds a bit unrealistic, but as with all worthwhile endeavors.. it is very realistic if you are willing to do the work and be resourceful. You can do a bit of research and hunt around for a few bargains, and come up with quality materials at prices well below normal if you are persistent and have time to wait for good deals as they become available.

I will start this chapter by showing you a fireplace below that my son and I built for under $1000.00

Yes... this fireplace was built for well under $1000.00!

How?? ...OK... lets break it down.

We gathered all of the rocks for free, about 2 pick-up truck loads. Just factor in your gas and lunch expense. Some rock quarries will let you pick up a couple of loads of rocks for very little if you simply tell them you will be using them as a training project. Indeed it will be just that.

You can also use a cultured or manufactured rock product that is made by several companies. These are much easier to work with than natural rock and since they are made with natural ingredients... they look very real, and have been used in some very high end Log Cabins. The draw back is that they will increase the cost of your $1000.00 Fireplace to around $2500.00 or more.

Now you will need to pick out your fireplace insert.

You can find a good used one on craigslist.org in your area like we did.

You will then want to frame up your fireplace with 2x4 material. After your 2x4 framing is complete, you will want to cover the framing with sheets of OSB (Oriented Strand Board). This will ad strength and give your screws a much better anchor. Then you will need a concrete skin, made up of sheets of Wonder Board or Durarock . They are made of lightweight concrete, and they generally come in 3'x4' sheets and are approx. 1/2" thick. You will then also screw them in place to completely cover the OSB. You should also plan to use deck screws for your fireplace framing instead of nails, and a product like liquid nails applied between the Concrete sheets, OSB, and framing studs for extra strength as well.

NOTE: The added step of gluing between all materials, will keep the Framework of your Fireplace from flexing too much. This in turn will help to prevent the mortar from cracking, and simply cut down on additional maintenance.

When framing your fireplace, install a 2"x 8"x 3" board where your mantel will be. This will be used to carry the weight of your Log Mantel. (2) - 2"x8" screwed together will do just fine. You will simply drill holes in the board for 1" pieces of Plumbing pipe, about 15" long. These pipes should be a little bit larger (1/16th") than the holes your are drilling to make a tight fit. Use a polyurethane glue such as "Gorilla Glue" to glue the pipes in place. Don't be afraid to let the pipes stick out through the back side of the board a little.

Then two short logs about 7-8" in diameter will be drilled with a wood auger to allow the logs to slide over the pipes. Don't drill all the way through...in fact, your 1" pipes should only sick out the front about 12-13" so only drill in about 12 - 13". Dry fit them to make sure they will go on tight. Then squirt some "Gorilla Glue" into the holes you have drilled and slide them on to the pipes. When you are ready to lay your rock, you will choose rocks that will fit around these logs.

The two logs that support your mantel log should be approx 16-18" long to start with. If you want to trim them later, be sure to note how far the pipes stick out to avoid cutting into them.

Plan to use a 4" grinder with a soft wheel, and a 36 grit sanding disc to round over the log ends and clean up the surface of the logs.

For the hearth you will want to frame it approx. 14" high if you want to sit on it later. Once your framing is completed you will be ready for your concrete skin. Apply the concrete skin to completely cover all exposed wood.

NOTE: Keep in mind that while this method makes a much lighter fireplace overall... it can still be heavy and you will want to plan to add some support under it to carry the extra weight.

To avoid getting your framing too hot, you will want to design the cavity that your fireplace insert sets in, to be lined with a concrete skin, made up of sheets of Wonder board or Dura-rock . You will then also screw them in place. Use the installation guide or contact a fireplace shop to get guidelines on how much free space should be between the concrete skin and your fireplace insert. If you choose to use a Gas Log insert this will be less of a concern.

You will want to plan to frame for the hardware used to install the insulated stove pipe for your chimney as well, This pipe will not be seen because it will be installed inside your framing, although you may want to install some extra concrete board to help insulate the exposed wood from heat. You will also want to install a couple of small vent registers at the bottom and the top of your fireplace. This will allow trapped heat to escape your chimney cavity and avoid fire danger. You can also simply fit your rocks around some holes or slots to make it look better instead of using the metal vent registers.

I recommend choosing the position of your rocks wisely, and remember that you will want to put some of them in your fireplace design simply just for character!. So don't be afraid to let a few smaller rocks stick out from the rest.

Go ahead and get your gas or wood fireplace installed after the framing is done but before you apply the outside concrete board. Here is a good schematic to assist you in your framing and insert installation.

Pellet and Wood insert: *http://www.thelinco.com/documents/Thelinco%20T-5000%20Fireplace%20Insert%20Manual.pdf*

Gas or Propane Insert: *http://www.lennoxhearthproducts.com/*

Gas or Propane Insert:
http://www.arcat.com/arcatcos/cos32/arc32505.html

Mortar and Rocks

This is the process that will make up the personality or character of your Rock Fireplace. This is where the fun begins so take your time and it will come out very nice.

I recommend that you go to Lowe's or Home Depot and pick up the pre-mixed sacks of mortar mix. for the fireplace above we used about (7) sacks at a cost of approx. $5.00 per sack. You will want to use a wheelbarrow to mix your rock mortar in, so you can mix outside and then wheel it in. Just mix (1) sack at a time to about the consistency of soft Peanut Butter. Don't mix it too dry or it will not hold the Rocks. Don't mix it too wet or it will take too long to dry.

Start by cleaning as many rocks as your mortar will go with. (About 6-10 rocks at a time) Scrub each one of your rocks with a scrub brush and some water. Be careful to get the surface that will be against the mortar... a bit cleaner.

Try to plan where you will place your rocks, and mock up two or three of them to make sure you like the fit. Keep a squirt bottle of water handy to spritz the rocks, and the concrete board. When you are ready to lay your first rocks, start with the hearth first, and plan to use some larger rocks that will be comfortable to sit on.

Simply spritz the area you will place your rock, and the rock itself. Using a large mortar trowel apply about a 1"deep application of mortar to the back surface of the rock you want to mortar in place. Then put the rock in place and jiggle it into place to create a vacuum or suction. Then just place another rock next to it, and so on. When you have about 3-4 rocks in place, go back and begin to fill the in the gaps with more mortar. you should space your rocks about 1"to 2" apart depending on the shape and look you want.

NOTE: When you begin to mortar the vertical rocks in place... you will want to use several 2x4 studs to hold them in place for up to 20 minutes until they begin to stay in place without sliding downward. Use more rocks to hold the base of the studs so they don't kick out. Sometimes it may be necessary to stand there and hold the rock in place until it will stay put on it's own. It is very helpful to go ahead and mortar in the gaps between the rocks to help them stay in place. Don't be tempted to mix your mortar too dry as it will not create the bond that you need to keep the rocks in place.

Make sure that you clean your rocks as you go because it will require much more effort to clean the rocks later if your don't.

Take your time and even if you are inexperienced it still should only take you about 16 man hours to do all of your mortaring, and about the same to frame and install your insert.

If it takes longer, so be it... The end result is a beautiful fireplace that you will enjoy for years to come, and it will be a center piece to your great room, living room, or basement family room!

Fireplace Summary:

Cost for Rocks - Free!... go to the river, rock quarry, or where ever there are rocks to be found for free.

Cost for Framing materials - OSB, glues, mortar mix, and concrete board all should not cost more than $ 300.00

Balance of $700.00 to apply to your insert, and insulated chimney components.

NOTE: As I mentioned we found our good used gas insert on www.craigslist.org and we bought it for $175.00 and we didn't need to spend the money to vent it because it is the "vent less" type of fireplace insert.

We did need to purchase the Black Gas Piping, Yellow Gas Pipe thread sealer tape, a Gas Regulator, and other fittings that cost altogether about $150.00

Check with your local building inspector for any Code requirements to factor in.

SUMMARY

We trust that you have begun to realize how do-able it is to build your own Log Cabin. You should never be afraid to attempt this if you have a little time and patience, and a desire to see it through... you will look back with great satisfaction, and enjoy the Log Cabin Lifestyle for years to come! Our websites are... TheLogHomeGuide.com, LogCabinHousePlans.net, and HowToBuildALogCabin.com

If you ever get stuck, simply email us at: **logpro1@gmail.com**

This ebook copyrighted 2006-2014 all rights reserved. This ebook may not be reproduced in any way, either electronically, photocopied, graphically, or otherwise. This ebook is published by HANDSCO

Copyright© 2006 - 2014 by Rob Winters

http://www.HowToBuildALogCabin.com

Author: Rob Winters

A PRODUCT OF THE UNITED STATES OF AMERICA

NOTES

Printed in Poland
by Amazon Fulfillment
Poland Sp. z o.o., Wrocław